Civil War Leaders

Wendy Conklin, M.A.

Table of Contents

Brave Leaders

During the Civil War many men became well-known leaders. They came from all walks of life. Some had been professors and others had been farmers. Many were professional soldiers or **politicians** (pol-uh-TISH-uhnz). Hundreds of officers died in battle. Others became heroes. These men were the best each side had to offer.

▼ Northern generals

▼ Southern generals

The Union Army

The **Union** army of the North had many advantages over the **Confederate** (kuhn-FED-uhr-uht) army from the South. The North had more men to serve as soldiers. For every three men in the Union army, there was only one man in the Confederate army. The North also had more factories and could produce more **ammunition** (am-yuh-NISH-uhn). Supplies were easily moved using the railroads in the North. The northern army had plenty of guns, clothing, and blankets. Their food supply was larger, too.

The Anaconda Plan

Early in the war, General Winfield Scott devised a plan to beat the South. He proposed to cut off all supplies going to the South. This plan was named after the anaconda snake that squeezes its enemy to death.

Ambrose Burnside

Burnside's Sideburns

Did you know that General Ambrose Burnside started the trend of growing long whiskers on the sides of men's cheeks? At first, these whiskers were called burnsides. Eventually they became known as sideburns.

In spite of all this, the North did have weaknesses. President Abraham Lincoln wanted to lead the army from his desk in Washington. He sent orders to the battlefields that the generals had to follow. This was frustrating for the generals.

Lincoln had trouble finding a leader that he thought could do a good job. Some of the northern commanders were Winfield Scott, George McClellan, John Pope, Ambrose Burnside, Joseph Hooker, George Meade, and Ulysses Grant.

Joseph Hooker

George McClellan

George Meade

The Commander in Chief

In November 1860, Abraham Lincoln was elected as the sixteenth president of the United States. The word united did not describe the United States at that time. For a very long time, the Southerners and the Northerners had disagreed about how to run the country.

The Politician

In his first speech as president, Lincoln said he would not abolish (uh-BOL-ish), or end, slavery in the slave states. He said this because he wanted to keep the country together.

The people in the South wanted the state governments to make the major decisions. For example, Southerners believed each state should decide whether or not to have slavery. Northerners believed the federal government should be more involved.

Lincoln spoke out against slavery. He said that slaves should have all the rights included in the Declaration of Independence. But Lincoln's main concern was keeping the nation together. Before he moved into the White House, seven states had **seceded** (suh-SEED-ed) from the Union. These states formed a new country called the Confederate States of America, or the CSA.

Allowing Slavery in the Union

The **Border States** were the slave states that bordered free states. During the Civil War, most of these states remained with the Union. This means they did not secede with the other slave states. The Border States were Delaware, Maryland, Kentucky, and Missouri.

Lincoln had to convince people in the North to go to war. He also had to make sure the North won the war. To do this he needed good generals, and they were hard to find. Lincoln gave the orders and expected the generals to follow. The generals did not always obey the president. Lincoln was still blamed for each loss.

Ulysses S. Grant

Ulysses S. Grant was a graduate of West Point. This was the most well-known military school at the time. He served in the Mexican War and then went into the business world.

No one really expected much of Grant when the Civil War began. But, Grant was a determined leader. He knew how to stand his ground and defeat his enemy in battle.

A Four-Star Rating

In 1864, Grant was given the title of lieutenant general. George Washington had also had such a high rank. Two years later, Grant was made a four-star general. This was the first time in history that Congress gave a general that many stars.

▲ General Grant at the Battle of Vicksburg in 1863

He was successful at the Battle of Shiloh in Tennessee. He held Vicksburg, Mississippi, under **siege** (SEEJ) for almost a year. Grant then took Chattanooga, Tennessee, from the South in November 1863.

In early 1864, Lincoln named him the commander of the entire northern army. Just over a year later, the war was over. Grant met General Robert E. Lee at Appomattox (ap-uh-MAT-uhks) Court House to accept the final **surrender** (suh-REN-duhr) of the Confederate army.

Sadly, it seems that fighting battles was the only thing that Grant did well. After the war, the American people elected him as the eighteenth president. His two terms were filled with **scandals**.

The March to the Sea

William T. Sherman was most likely the smartest commander for the North. Sherman was both a brilliant and a risky leader. He moved quickly and sometimes even left behind supplies as his men chased the Confederate army. He allowed his troops to eat whatever they wanted off the farms in the South. Sherman and his soldiers were very successful on the battlefield.

The Christmas Present

Just before Christmas in 1864, Sherman's army took control of Savannah, Georgia. Sherman sent President Lincoln a telegram. The telegram presented Savannah with its 150 guns and 25,000 bales of cotton as a Christmas gift to the president.

General Sherman was a strong Union leader.

▲ Sherman's men tore up railroad tracks across the South.

Sherman's army is best known for its 1864 "March to the Sea." Sherman believed in "Total War." He thought that the fastest way to win the war was to totally destroy the South. The southern soldiers would want to end the war faster if they knew their homes were being destroyed.

Sherman's Neckties

Some of the southern railroad ties were heated in the center and wrapped around trees. People called them "Sherman's Neckties" because they looked like neckties around the trees.

Sherman's army dug up parts of the railroad in the South. This prevented the southern army from receiving their supplies. The Northerners marched through Georgia and the Carolinas burning and destroying everything. Every barn, house, and field in their way went up in flames. Many people in the South said, "We will never forgive him for this!"

More Northern Leaders

General George McClellan was one of the first commanders of the northern army. President Lincoln chose him to replace the aging Winfield Scott. McClellan's soldiers liked him, but he often froze on the battlefield.

General George Meade is probably best known for his command at the Battle of Gettysburg. He never performed brilliant **maneuvers** (muh-NEW-vuhrz) in battle. But, he was reliable and knew how to hold his ground. At Gettysburg, he led the North to one of its biggest victories.

Just before Gettysburg, Lincoln offered General John Reynolds command of the army. Reynolds gracefully declined the offer. He died on the first day of the Battle at Gettysburg. His job was to hold off the enemy until the rest of the northern army arrived. He succeeded, but he paid with his life.

Custer Makes His Debut

George Custer is best known for the Battle of Little Bighorn in 1876, but he first fought in the Civil War. In fact, his men received a Confederate flag of truce just before Lee surrendered the whole army at Appomattox.

George Custer

One interesting northern **regiment** (REJ-uh-muhnt) was the 54th Massachusetts. Black soldiers and a white commander named Robert Shaw made up this regiment. At Fort Wagner, South Carolina, they led a heroic **bayonet** (bay-uh-NET) charge. Many men died and some suffered terrible wounds. Their bravery earned the respect of many people.

▼ The 54th Massachusetts lead the bayonet charge at Fort Wagner.

Philip Sheridan

A War Maker

Philip Sheridan was often described as a ruthless war maker. He led soldiers under General Grant and swept the enemy away in battle.

The Rebels

The Southerners were fighting for states' rights. They seceded from the Union because they wanted to set up their own government. Southerners wanted each state to decide about slavery. The people in the South were tired of the United States government telling them what to do. So, they formed a new country called the Confederate States of America. It was also known as the **Confederacy** (kuhn-FED-er-uh-see).

The South had many advantages in this war. First of all, the South had skilled fighters and excellent generals. Many of these men were trained to fight in the Mexican War. They were professional soldiers. There were also thousands of farmers who knew how to use their guns. They were used to riding horses and liked the outdoors. Another advantage was that the Southerners were defending their land.

The biggest problem for the South was its economy. The region did not have enough money for all the supplies they would need. They did not have many railroad routes already

Let the South Go

Some people in the North wanted to let the South secede. They said the United States did not need the South. Instead, these people wanted to focus on making the United States stronger with just the northern states.

Confederate Money

When the South formed the Confederacy, they needed a money system. The CSA started printing Confederate bills. This currency was never worth very much.

built and most of the factories were in the North. An army could not survive on the food from **plantations** (plan-TAY-shuhnz) alone. They needed more resources, like weapons, to succeed.

▼ A cotton plantation on the Mississippi River

The Other President

Like many other young men at this time, Jefferson Davis attended the West Point Military Academy. He served his country by fighting in the Mexican War. He was a very smart man and served in both houses of Congress. When the Confederate States of America was formed, Davis seemed like the perfect leader for the South. He was chosen as the president of the new country.

However, Davis did not like to share control. He appointed every general for the southern army. He also had trouble trusting people who worked with him. Because he was so controlling, many people did not like him much.

In Search of a Job

When the South seceded, Davis hoped that they would name him commander in chief of their armies. He thought his experiences from West Point and the army would make him a great candidate. Instead, they named him president.

Jefferson Davis served as president of the CSA.

Jefferson Davis in his prison cell after the Civil War

Jail Time

When the war ended, Davis tried to hide. Northerners captured him a month later. He was put in prison for two years. Some people in the Union thought that Davis was involved in President Lincoln's **assassination** (uh-sas-uh-NAY-shuhn). Davis denied that he had anything to do with the president's death.

His army needed supplies badly, but he could not make the people in the Confederacy pay taxes. Each southern state acted independently and made their own laws. The states had their own money and their own leaders.

Davis believed that foreign countries would join the Southerners because the southern plantations traded valuable crops to Europe. But, he was unable to persuade other countries to help the South in the war. Most European countries did not think the South could win. No one wanted to fight for the losing side. Unfortunately for the Confederacy, Davis did not get the help the South needed.

A Truly Great General

Perhaps the greatest general on either side during the war was Robert E. Lee. Lee was a Virginian. Both the Union and Confederate armies wanted Lee to serve. He truly loved his home state and did not want to fight against Virginia. After thinking about his decision, he chose to join the southern army.

Beginning the War

At the beginning of the war, President Abraham Lincoln offered Lee the command of the Union army. Lee turned the United States president down. Instead, he became the Confederate president's military advisor.

Lee was a great leader. He understood and could plan brilliant military **strategies** (STRAT-uh-geez). He inspired his officers and his soldiers to fight and die for the southern cause.

Lee believed in charging at the enemy quickly and with force. Time and time again his army beat an army more than twice its size. He won battle after battle until July 1863 when he suffered a terrible defeat at the Battle of Gettysburg. At the same time, Vicksburg fell in Mississippi. In 1864, Lee's army could not hold off the Northerners at Petersburg and Richmond. Once the Northerners controlled the Confederate capital city of Richmond, Lee knew the war was ending.

Traveller the Horse

Lee's horse, Traveller, was the most well-known horse in all of the Civil War. Newspaper reports and photos of Lee mounted on him made Traveller a celebrity in both the North and the South.

When it appeared that all the supplies had run out, Lee surrendered to General Ulysses S. Grant. The two great men met in a home in Appomattox Court House, Virginia. Lee held his head high, wore his best uniform, and agreed to the surrender. He told his men to go home to their families. The war was over.

Thomas "Stonewall" Jackson

Thomas Jackson was a graduate of West Point. He served in the Mexican War. After that war, he became a professor. His students did not like him in the classroom, but his men loved him on the battlefield.

During the Civil War, Jackson led his men to victory against all odds. General Robert E. Lee called Jackson his "right arm." That meant that Lee always wanted Jackson nearby, and Lee trusted Jackson.

At the First Battle of Bull Run, Jackson's men were facing heavy fire from the northern army. A southern soldier saw him and said, "There is Jackson standing like a stone wall." Some people think this was a compliment. Others believe that the soldier felt that Jackson should have been marching forward rather than just standing. After the battle, soldiers in the North and South called him "Stonewall Jackson." This name was considered a compliment for a brave leader.

At the Battle of Chancellorsville in Virginia, Jackson was accidentally shot by one of his own men. The wound

Thomas Jackson

was so bad that the doctor had to remove Jackson's left arm. Just as it seemed he was getting better, he caught **pneumonia** (new-MOAN-yuh) and died. The entire southern army mourned this **irreplaceable** (ear-ruh-PLAY-suh-buhl) man.

▼ Map of the Bull Run area showing the 1861 battle

His Final Orders

As Jackson lay dying, he called out these final words, "Prepare for action. Let us cross the river and rest under the shade of the trees."

More Southern Leaders

The Confederate army had other great officers. General James Longstreet was a large man. General Lee affectionately called Longstreet, "my old war horse." Longstreet's ideas on war were ahead of his time. He believed in defensive warfare. He spent time trying to convince Lee to dig in rather than charging.

General George Pickett longed for a good fight. He finally got his chance at the Battle of Gettysburg. It was there that Pickett led a famous charge on the final day of battle. Later, he blamed Lee for the terrible charge that took nearly all of his men.

▼ Pickett's charge at the Battle of Gettysburg

J.E.B. Stuart was Lee's "eyes and ears of the army." He commanded the **cavalry** (KAV-uhl-ree). However, instead of **scouting** the enemy and reporting to Lee, Stuart liked to take long rides. He and his men raided Union camps and tried to get their names in the papers. Stuart's fun cost the South greatly at Gettysburg. At that time, Lee did not know where the northern army was located.

It was the leaders who made the biggest impact on the soldiers during the war. Many of these leaders led by rallying their men. Both the North and the South had men who gave everything they had on the battlefields. While some proved to be better leaders than others, they all inspired the men who served under them.

▲ General J.E.B. Stuart's cavalry scouting in 1862

Longstreet and Grant

Generals Longstreet and Grant were good friends going back to their days at West Point and the Mexican War. Longstreet even attended Grant's wedding. After Grant's death, Longstreet said, "Grant was the truest, as well as the bravest man that ever lived."

Glossary

abolish—to end

ammunition—supply of bullets and shells for guns or cannons

assassination—when someone is killed for political reasons

bayonet—a blade attached to the end of a rifle

Border States—slave states that bordered free states

cavalry—soldiers who ride horses in battle and are often scouts

Confederacy—the Confederate States of America; the states that seceded from the Union

Confederate—a person who supported the South in the Civil War; comes from the name of the country formed by the states that seceded, the Confederate States of America

economy—the activities of an area that have to do with money

irreplaceable—cannot be replaced

maneuvers—planned movements of soldiers during battles

plantations—large farms that produced crops for money

pneumonia—sickness in which the lungs fill with fluid

politicians—people who run for and serve in political offices

regiment—a unit of the army that can be divided into several smaller troops

scandals—behaviors that lead to people thinking you have low moral values

scouting—secretly getting information about the opposing side in a battle

seceded—pulled out or withdrew from something; states that left the Union

siege—a military blockade of an area that cuts off all contact with the outside world

strategies—plans for how to succeed in battle

surrender—to give up and lose a battle or the war

Union—term used to describe the United States of America; also the name given to the northern army during the Civil War